Goodnight, Africa

How Changing Other's Lives Can Change Your Own

Cindy D. Whitmer

BALBOA.
PRESS
A DIVISION OF HAY HOUSE

Interior Graphics/Art Credit: Debbie Galbraith & John Bishop

Balboa Press books may be ordered through booksellers or by contacting:

Balboa Press
A Division of Hay House
1663 Liberty Drive
Bloomington, IN 47403
www.balboapress.com
1 (877) 407-4847

Print information available on the last page.

ISBN: 978-1-5043-7272-5 (sc)
ISBN: 978-1-5043-7273-2 (hc)
ISBN: 978-1-5043-7274-9 (e)

Library of Congress Control Number: 2016921541

Balboa Press rev. date: 01/13/2017

This book is lovingly dedicated to John Bishop, who believed I had something to offer, invited me to join the team & then "adopted" me.

And to Debbie Galbraith, my closest travel companion, tent-mate, and dearest friend.

With Deep Appreciation to the rest of the Kansas to Kenya Community Team:

Joe Bob Lake
Nyakio Kaniu-Lake
Jennifer Allen
Bob Basow
Nancy Cohn
Donna Griffin
Sandy Procter
Fran Wheeler
Dean Wolfe

Written with love and appreciation for all my new found brothers and sisters in Africa.

Thanks, Dad

Acknowledgments

First of all, I wish to thank DeAnna May for her patience, humor and kindness in helping me choose the team at Balboa Press and "starting the engine." Secondly, I want to thank my project coordinator, John Ocampo, for his persistence, consistency, patience, and guidance throughout the creation of this book. I am equally grateful to the rest of the Balboa Press team who have worked meticulously to put my written words and vision into physical form.

A big thank you to the Abundant Life Center congregation in St. Joseph, Missouri, for your spontaneous and generous donations for the firewood fees for the African children. I also greatly appreciate your prayers and support for my safety, health, and success while I was traveling.

Special thanks to my son, Justin Whitmer, for watching over our home and my beloved new kitten, Pebble, while I was away. Your presence there truly comforted me.

Special thanks to my daughter, Laura Whitmer, for offering her editorial advice and comments. You truly strengthened this book in amazing ways and taught me so much!

To both of my children, thank you so much for always supporting me when I make "yet another decision" or take "yet another trip."

Because you both take the time to truly know and understand me, I hope you always see by my example how life is an amazing adventure and the possibilities are endless for anyone willing to open themselves up to interesting, fun, and meaningful experiences.

I am blessed beyond measure with deep, loving, supportive friendships from many all over the globe. At this particular moment in my life, I wish to thank Jill Myers, Debbie Galbraith, Michelle Kaplan, Brooke Johnson, Tresa Leftenant, Jean Schoeneker, Teresa Merrill, Sheri Kwapiszeski, Adam Buhman-Wiggs, and Kathi Wells for our extraordinary connections and histories which have survived and thrived through many seasons and circumstances. You are each very unique players in my universe, and I really cannot imagine life without you in it. Thank you so much for the diverse ways you have supported, encouraged, and lifted me up over the years.

To John Bishop, without whom, this trip nor this book would ever have happened. Every time I have a cup of Out of Africa Tea, I think of you. (Was that part of your plan?)

And most of all, I am grateful for the Divine Love that guides and directs my life, offering love to every situation, igniting passion in my soul, warmth in my heart, and certainty in my mind that all is well no matter what.

"Travel is fatal to prejudice, bigotry, and narrow-mindedness, and many of our people need it sorely on these accounts. Broad, wholesome, charitable views of men and things cannot be acquired by vegetating in one little corner of the earth all one's lifetime."
~ Mark Twain

"Traveling - it leaves you speechless,
then turns you into a storyteller."
~ Ibn Battuta

Introduction

Since my children went off to college, I have been living a "Bucket List" kind of life. Quitting my job, putting my house on the market, and packing my car, I traveled around the Eastern part of the United States for three months. Because my house hadn't sold, I returned to it for the holiday season.

Shortly after, I attended a local community holiday event and delighted in mixing with many of the business people I had been living and working in town with for the past several years.

As was our tradition, John Bishop and I spoke politely with one another, updating each other on our lives. We have been acquaintances for many years with mutual respect and a shared sense of humor.

While we were visiting, he mentioned he had heard I'd been traveling quite extensively. He generously acknowledged he knew I had done wonderful work at our local counseling center for many years and had gathered I was quite a spiritual person from reading the column I used to write for the newspaper.

After this array of compliments, he slid right into introducing me to K2K, the Kansas to Kenya nonprofit organization he has been involved with for many years, and wanted to know if I would consider becoming a member of the community team and go on the next mission trip in June 2016.

My jaw dropped. If I had any cheese and crackers left in my mouth, I would have choked on them. What? Me? You want ME to go to Africa to help people? What in the world do I have to offer the African people?

The following week we met to more extensively discuss the purpose of the organization, the logistics of the trip, and how he saw me serving the people. When I arrived, a beautiful spread of photos from his last several trips were before me, helping me instantly fall in love with the people and the idea. (John is a smart man.)

Then he explained that after our mission work was accomplished, we would spend the final two days in Africa playing as a team by going on safari and taking a hippo tour.

Remember how I mentioned I'm a "Bucket List" person? Well, on my list has always been, "Go on a mission trip," "Go to Africa," and "Go on Safari." Wow! Even though I told John at the end of our meeting that day that I was going to take the month to think about it, deep inside my heart I was hearing myself (or perhaps someone else) saying, "Yes!"

Six months later, it was time to go.

Day 1

I am leaving behind Pebble (a seven-month-old kitten I adopted less than two weeks ago), everyone I know, my entire worldly possessions, and my country. I am going to Africa.

How is it that I find myself, having just recently turned forty-nine, getting numerous vaccinations, dropping thousands of dollars, and spending hours and hours learning about a culture so beautiful but so troubled?

In Africa, five dollars will pay an entire year firewood fee which provides one student a cooked meal every day at school. Absurd! What in America can I get for my children that lasts more than a day for five dollars? Eight to ten people live in houses with one or two tiny rooms. In America, we build three thousand-square foot homes with three garages and still need additional storage for all our material possessions.

Our worlds appear very different, but I have a deep suspicion I will come to see that we are far more alike than we seem.

For now, I must force myself to walk away from all I've known, leave my comfort zone, and part from the newest love of my life, Pebble.

I have already parted from my human children (now young adults) as they left a week ago on vacation with their father. Imagining being half a world away from them does not make me comfortable either. After all, I had refused all opportunities to leave the country without them throughout their childhood years. However, it is in the stretching of ourselves that we grow, learn, and use our experiences to serve others.

This is always my intention.

John picked me up, and on his arrival, I dragged my bags and my body out the door while glancing back at my new kitten with some despair. John's smile, hug, and immediate assistance with my bags reminded me I was not alone, and everything was going to be all right. The drive to KCI (Kansas City International Airport) was smooth and pleasant as I participated in polite conversation with him and his lovely wife, Marge.

After I agreed to go on this mission trip, I fell and shattered one of my wrists into nineteen pieces, which required surgery and several months of healing and rehabilitation. One of my concerns was I didn't want anyone to have to manage my luggage for me. Therefore, I felt a sense of victory when we arrived, and I was able to roll both of my fifty-pound suitcases behind me and carry my backpack by myself. Mission accomplished.

Weigh-in and check-in went smoothly. We crammed in as many gifts for the Kenyan people as possible, leaving little room for our personal items. I wondered about some of the items we packed for them, like toothbrushes. Why were these particular things chosen? We also took books for two libraries, soccer uniforms, soccer balls, hats, and prizes. We would purchase lots of food, school supplies, mosquito nets, and other necessities when we arrived.

Debbie and I were the newest team members but have been close friends for nearly two decades. We stuck close to each other, using the buddy system. After we checked our bags, we thought we were being helpful by moving down to security and getting to our gate. Pretty soon, her phone rang. It was Joe Bob, our team leader, wondering where we had wandered off to. Oops. We were supposed to wait for everyone before moving to the gate. There's always someone in a group causing trouble … I just didn't think it would be me!

Before too long, we were on our way and had a quick, easy flight to Detroit, Michigan, just in time for our five-hour layover.

Walking around the airport, we perused the food choices for the "last supper." Realizing we would be sitting for many hours in the next day, we made several rounds back and forth. We entertained ourselves by people-watching and scanning the shops.

Eventually, we settled on Qdoba, a Mexican restaurant, to tide us over. As I thoroughly enjoyed my tacos, a musician dressed in a tux just a few feet away played delightful classical music on a grand piano. Fancy entertainment and ambience were paired with a couple of basic tacos and down-to-earth conversation with my travel partners.

Underneath it though, I realized these were my last precious hours in the United States, and the next time I stepped on American soil I would be a changed woman. I also hoped I would have changed some things for my Kenyan brothers and sisters.

Day 2

On board the red-eye from Detroit, Michigan, to Amsterdam, Holland, Debbie and I were in the last row of the plane with no ability to recline our seats for the eight-hour flight. We found this a bit inconvenient and uncomfortable, but then I remembered there were people starving where we were headed, and I quickly regained perspective.

The flight was fine, food was good, I rested some, visited some, and read a bit. All in all, it was pleasant and uneventful.

We geared up to make a quick transfer to our final flight with no time whatsoever to bask in the uniqueness of the Amsterdam airport or even remember that we were technically in Europe. I regretfully walked quickly by a Dutch chocolate food store, pretending I didn't want to stop — yum — and just kept focused on finding Gate F3, Nairobi bound. At least I got to go to the bathroom.

I think this was my favorite flight. The staff, based out of Amsterdam, was particularly hospitable, friendly, and attentive.

We were fed well every three hours or so. I wish I had taken pictures of the meals, as I hadn't been fed for real on a flight in years, and never like this! Pasta, salad, rolls, and dessert. Cheese was always involved. Pizza, pesto, raspberry with chocolate and some kind of cream. Delicious.

The flight attendants delivered a smile with every meal. And then, moments later, offered coffee, tea, or water. So much comfort in their presence and care. It felt quite ironic to have our basic needs so thoroughly met on an airplane that was taking us to a place where the people were in desperate need of everything.

I slept some, read some, got to know some of my fellow travelers more, and just relaxed as much as possible.

My favorite moment was when we saw Africa coming into view out the window, with the beautiful green and blue seashore outlining the desert, barren regions of the North. The contrast was striking. I couldn't keep my eyes off this masterful painting.

Africa is huge, and much of the northern part looks dry, arid, and uninhabited. Later, we crossed the line from light to dark, so I rested once more.

In Africa, we are eight hours ahead of where we came. It was late evening there when we landed.

On arrival, the first agenda item was purchasing our visa, which required two forms, fingerprints, thumbprints, passport, fifty dollars, and a photo. The line was long. I was tired and running out of steam.

Next we proceeded to baggage claim. Waiting for my bags to pop up on the carousel seemed like an eternity. We had traveled nearly thirty hours. Where were the bags?

Luckily, all pieces of our group's luggage arrived safely. Next, we dragged everything through Customs. Pressing forward with what little energy remained, I was pleasantly surprised this only required one form and a few standard questions. No big deal. In a few short steps, I realized we had exited the airport.

We found our bus and were told not to take photos of the airport or anything around it for security reasons. (You are not in Kansas anymore, Dorothy/Cindy.)

We were struck by the restricted-items sign that included standards any seasoned traveler would expect, like knives. However, this one included elephant tusks, ninja swords, rhinoceros horns, and other local possibilities. Wow! We really are on a different continent. Just from the sight of this sign, I felt my brain expanding and my heart opening wider as it reminded me how big and diverse our world is.

In Nairobi, we found out our first bus driver's name was David, which struck me as funny, as it is such a common name in America. He was kind and a confident driver. He let me sit up front. Even though darkness had fallen, I saw beautiful trees and many signs in English. This surprised and comforted me.

Finally, we arrived at the hotel. We had to show passports and sign forms again, but at last were allowed to settle into our rooms for the night.

Exhausted and unsure how I would get through the next two weeks, I turned on the shower. The water was brown at first. The "hot" water was lukewarm at best, so I got goose bumps and decided to totally skip shaving and washing my long, thick hair.

The toilet didn't flush properly, either. Ugh.

Just go to sleep, Cindy.

Goodnight, Africa.

Day 3

As has been my experience, life always looks better after sleeping. Having rested well, we got organized and headed to breakfast. Eager for a freshly made omelet, my enthusiasm dipped a bit when I realized there wasn't any cheese. So, eggs and veggies it was! The rest of my meal included potatoes, mango juice, hot tea, and *chapati*, an African staple at nearly every meal. Considered bread, chapati reminded me of tortillas most of all.

Gazing out the dining room window, I noticed an African gentleman making a music video with backup singers and all. The grounds surrounding the hotel were lovely, natural, and inviting.

Wanting to be a helpful team member, I diligently ate my breakfast and headed back up to the room to be all packed in time to go. Pretty quickly, I realized we were now on "Africa time" (slower, looser) which is completely different from how we type-A Americans function. Perhaps we were to be in the lobby by ten o'clock, but we didn't go anywhere until noon.

Patience would be a necessity on this trip, but at this point I had no idea how much so.

Even though our toilet never flushed properly, we managed. The morning schedule was quite relaxed, offering us some turnaround time I suppose, and we filled it by enjoying the grounds, visiting, journaling, and contemplating everything that was to come.

We met some Kenyans, all of whom were kind, helpful, and friendly. They seemed proud of their land and culture despite their problems.

Nyakio, our team leader originally from Kenya, introduced us to her nieces. In them, we saw children with wealth in Africa: nice clothes, good education, and access to lots of opportunities. They were smart and well-spoken.

First stop of the day was YaYa (the mall) in Nairobi to exchange money and get prepaid phones for the team. Everything had high security and took time. I practiced <u>major</u> patience, but everyone was kind. Transitioning into another country was a process, for sure.

We had delicious smoothies for lunch and learned that the equivalent of one dollar is a big tip for waitresses because the average daily salary in Kenya equals three dollars.

With more logistics taken care of, we were on to Lake Naivasha Crescent Camp which was to be our home for the majority of our time here. Along the way, we stopped at the Great Rift Valley Overlook, a beautiful, open, green-hilled area. Despite the cloudy, misty weather, we took advantage of the photo opportunity. Here, I realized I was south of the Equator for the first time in my life, standing in the Southern Hemisphere of the Earth.

We browsed the little shops while the workers followed us around closely doing everything they could to get us to buy. I didn't. I was a bit put off by the lack of personal space to look around, the absence of price tags, and the constant efforts to barter. Besides, the trip was my gift, and I didn't want to start spending money on gifts for others already.

As we traveled along, traffic seemed a bit crazy. Driving on the left side was disorienting in and of itself. We were on the AIDS highway, the only decent passageway across Kenya. Truck traffic was thick, and no one seemed to follow any protocol at all. The only traffic signals we saw in Africa were in Nairobi. Everywhere else appeared to be a free-for-all.

Along the way we got our first glimpse of rural Kenya filled with very tiny, poor communities with slum-like conditions. Tiny "shops" that looked like they could fall into themselves at any moment were everywhere with just a few products available. We were told most people lived without running water and electricity. How do they survive?

The realities in front of us greatly saddened me. I felt overwhelmed with wondering how I could possibly do anything to turn these circumstances around for my Kenyan brothers and sisters. Then all of a sudden we witnessed a family of baboons walking along the highway, six giraffes, and tons of cows, goats, and goat herders. My sadness switched to delight seeing the vast array of wildlife in my midst. Very cool moment for the animal fan in me!

By late afternoon, we arrived at Lake Naivasha Crescent Camp. The staff, who would soon become our friends, greeted us with warm washcloths to freshen up and pineapple juice to nourish us. As we delighted in this treatment, they also unloaded all of our very heavy bags and one thousand mosquito nets.

We received our tent assignments and were overjoyed with how spacious and lovely our accommodations were. The luxury tents were mounted on wood logs with screened windows on all sides that conveniently zipped open and closed. The floors were hardwood in the main area with two beautiful beds draped decoratively with mosquito nets. The room included a desk and chair in one corner, a sitting area with two soft chairs and a small table in the other corner, and each bed had an accompanying end table and light for our convenience.

Beyond the main living space was a large bathroom with an enclosed flushable toilet, a big shower, sink, counter, and other large area with a mirror for grooming with additional storage space for luggage. The whole tent was covered with a large canopy for additional protection from the elements. We quickly and easily settled in, finding a place for all of our personal items and claiming our individual spaces. As I placed my book, journal, pen, kleenex, water bottle and reading glasses on my bedside table, I felt at home. This was something familiar.

The natural surroundings of the camp were gorgeous! Beautiful, tall, yellow trees, native birds, Lake Naivasha, flowers of all colors and varieties, and plants galore were such a welcome site! Now officially tent mates, Debbie and I unpacked, explored the area, took lots of photos and found ourselves by the lake in conversation with two Kenyan men.

Having lost track of the time from visiting so long by the lake, we realized the electric fence closer to our tents had been shut for the night because when darkness falls, sometimes the hippos wander up on land. (Very territorial, hippopotamuses kill more humans than any other animal in Africa!)

As we rapidly looked for other routes available in case a hippo came charging out of the water, I thought to myself, "This is not how it's all gonna end for me." (Although, let's face it, it would have made a very unique death story!) Luckily, the Kenyan guys yelled loudly enough for help so a staff person heard and quickly opened the electric fence inviting us to safety. (I didn't know it then, but the threat of hippos charging was the only times I felt true anxiety and concern for my well-being on this entire journey.)

Crisis averted, we spent a bit more time settling into our new home then headed to the dining lodge for a delicious buffet style dinner with everyone together. Rolls, rice, potatoes, vegetables, steak, beans, banana flan, coffee, tea, and our own bottled water were spread across the serving tables. We were being spoiled I think.

One of our interns was having a birthday, so they brought out dessert while we all sang to her. Apparently cake, candles, and song are customary here, too.

After a lengthy team meeting, song practice for church the next day, and devotions, we were allowed to rest.

Much to our delight, our beds were warmed with hot water bottles. Also, the shower water was clear and hot. Hallelujah! What a huge blessing to be so comfortable! However, the wifi wasn't working yet and my cell phone signal was low, so texting the kids was out of the question. (These were the kinds of things we began to refer to as "First World Problems" as opposed to "Third World.")

As I began to drift off, I realized something. Here I was all snug and warm in my "tent" with more space and modern conveniences than the Kenyan people I came here to serve who lived just a few miles away. Also, I secretly wondered what the living conditions were like for the lovely men and women who were staff members at the camp. After they took such good care of us every day and maintained our comfortable accommodations, what kind of homes did they return to? This haunted me a bit. I had so much to learn and intended to.

As I closed my eyes, I secretly wished everyone would make traveling to other cultures a priority. I was already so grateful I had.

Goodnight, Africa.

Day 4

When I awoke, I realized it was Father's Day, so of course I thought of my dad immediately. Three years ago, he died unexpectedly at the age of sixty-nine. Because of that, I became even more determined to live fully without regrets, to embrace opportunities as they presented themselves, and not wait until "someday" for anything important to me. So I give him partial credit for me saying, "Yes" to this experience and was also blessed to use part of my inheritance to finance the trip. Thank you, Dad.

What a day in Africa it was! To my delight, it began with me hearing hippos bellowing in the night. Wow, that was a first for me!

Breakfast was tasty and satisfying. Then we rode off to St. John's Church for a day of worship and fellowship. The K2K organization helped this church building become a reality, and today it was consecrated. The celebration began outside the gate with all the congregants standing on the rough dirt road. After some ceremony including prayer, song, a message and cheering, we entered the gate together and circled the entire bright orange church, blessing it on every side. The grounds included a large tank to catch rain water, a garden, and open spaces for fellowship, play, and parking. However, most people walk everywhere because they don't have cars.

In addition to our team and the local congregants and ministers, Archbishop Moochi was there, along with visiting pastors from the area and a prominent citizen running for Parliament. We took communion, and forty candidates were confirmed. Different groups sang and danced. The power of their voices was unbelievable and their deep faith, obvious.

Even our group got involved singing a song for the congregation with joy and enthusiasm. Fran, our group chaplain, gave a brief sermon and assisted in the service as well. Hardly anyone spoke English, and yet we seemed to grasp what was happening.

People of all ages participated in the service. They chose some hymns common to us as well and gave us seats close to the front. Special privileges continued throughout our stay.

At one point in the service while children sang, I noticed a boy with a sling up front. There he stood, with a very simple wooden cast with only a narrow piece of white cloth used to hold it up to his side, hand-tied around his neck. Remembering my own fall four months before, I couldn't help but feel sympathy for him and compare our casts and slings. I'm sure I was given the highest quality available. His was humble at best. Would he heal as well as I had? How much unnecessary pain had he experienced? Guilt crept up as I realized my top notch cast and sling had just been gathering dust in my closet for the past couple of months and instead could have been passed along to this child for his comfort and healing.

After the service concluded, we were given the honor to plant a tree on the grounds, and then were treated to lunch with the privilege of a private room with the bishop and his wife. I realized I was not that comfortable being treated with prominence, as if anyone was beneath me, but the Kenyan people were so kind and hospitable. They wanted to do these things for us. I recognized the importance of allowing them to give back whatever they had to offer.

The most significant experience of the day for me was interacting with the children. From the moment we arrived, they stared at us, quite shyly really, so we broke the ice and talked to them.

They were very captivated with my hair, caressing it over and over while saying, "So soft, so long," and asked me what I did to make it that way. I chuckled while I admitted I just wash it every other day, and it's only because I am a *mzunga* (a white person) that it is textured like this.

They asked us about our families and what school is like in America. They told us about school there and some of their problems and dreams. One girl revealed that a man had slapped her right at the church. We didn't know who he was to the girl but all she said she did was touch a book without asking. What were we supposed to do with this information? If we attempted to talk to her mother or the man himself about the incident, would the girl be spared further abuse or perhaps would things get worse for her?

Another girl told me she dreams of opening a hospital someday where there isn't one and helping people. I told her and some others to decide in their minds what they really want, see it clearly, and not let any obstacles deter them. I wanted these girls to believe in themselves and not let boys, men, culture, or anything else get in their way. We danced with them after lunch and had such a good time.

They all admitted they wanted to come to the United States and asked us many questions about where we live and what everything is like. I found it difficult to describe the lifestyles of typical Americans in terms that they could relate to at all. Our conversations challenged and delighted me. Like children everywhere, their curiosity and wonder shined through their beautiful faces and bright eyes.

They wanted hugs when we were leaving. I gladly embraced them, called them by name, and told them I would remember them. Life in Kenya is not easy for girls or for anyone, really. As I witnessed the evidence of extreme poverty and listened to the people's stories, more and more I understood why we had come.

I knew I hadn't solved any of these complicated problems, but as we pulled out of the church parking lot I privately hoped my smile, praise, worshipful spirit, encouragement and compassionate heart, all had an impact on them. Otherwise, what would be the point of all this?

We rode back to camp. Church service lasted four hours and the fellowship went on for two more. Wow! (Where I come from, the Holy Spirit leaves at noon, so you better be finished!) But here, the people are rich in faith and truly reserve all of Sunday as God's day. Nothing else appears to matter outside of worship and fellowship. This is one of the qualities I admired most in these wonderful people. How our Sundays were filled in America would be shocking to this population, I was certain. (Watching the

NFL, kids' soccer games or piano recitals, completing household chores, or even going to work on a Sunday — that's America!)

On the way back, we saw zebras and waterbucks. The sun was shining, too, so the view of Mount Longonot was incredible as well as all the surrounding hills, trees, and valleys.

Traffic and being transported everywhere was quite unsettling. The best highway had two lanes and people used the lines as suggestions, not strict driving boundaries. Always busy, traffic included many trucks, sometimes donkeys, and several times trucks passing while heading straight toward another truck only to slip back in the line in the nick of time. This was not our driver being difficult. This was the culture. I stopped watching after a while and instead locked my eyes out the windows to view nature and the evidence of poverty all around it.

We returned to camp, rested just a bit, had a planning meeting for the week, then ate dinner. I felt eager to help out everywhere I could. I was impressed with this team which included ministers, an architect, a nutritionist, a nurse, business professionals, a teacher, and a social worker, many of whom have been coming here for years. I'm thankful they've allowed me to be a part of it and embraced me as one of them.

Goodnight, Africa.

Day 5

A beautiful chorus of birds and other animals woke us up. It was the most delightful alarm clock ever! Another nice breakfast consumed, off we went for the day. Our group split up and began the heart of the work we came to do.

John asked Debbie and me to go to Badilika (meaning: change/transformation) for the first half of the day. This was an addictions recovery center that John helped establish, as he is a recovered alcoholic. In addition to supporting them financially, he introduced the Twelve Steps of Alcoholics Anonymous to the locals. Holding John in high regard, they had painted his portrait on the wall inside.

We visited with Jose who runs the center, along with Charles, Chewy, Hussein, and James. James played guitar for us while we sang songs together, talked about politics, cultural issues, family life, and every subject you can imagine.

We were surprised they had such strong feelings about our upcoming presidential election and how the outcome of that would affect international relations. Amazed by their passionate opinions, I realized even more how our actions in the United States impact everyone around the world. Although these gentlemen had constant daily challenges, even sometimes unsure if they would eat, they still stayed interested and eager about greater world events. Impressive and surprising, indeed.

One of my new friends, whom I would have guessed was at least ten years older than me, asked me my age, then told me he was forty-eight, one year younger than me. Wow. Conditions in Kenya are difficult, and the life expectancy is currently fifty-nine for men and sixty-three for women, significantly lower than the United States. I learned this represented a great improvement in the past two decades, however.

All the gentlemen from Badilika were so kind. Eventually Jose took us to meet his wife Dorcas in their home, just a short walk (but through rocky, uneven, muddy terrain). Immediately I picked up his little daughter Percy but she was frightened, probably because I was white (he explained) and also too silly with her too quickly. She warmed up to me a bit eventually, but I felt sorry for making her uncomfortable.

Their home was modest and small by American standards but bigger and nicer than many in this part of the world. They rent their cozy place, and it had some security with a gate outside the row of attached homes.

Dorcas and Jose shared their story of meeting which led to marriage in a week! They seemed quite sweet on each other. Their other daughter Lucy is six, in school, with spina bifida. Dorcas carries her to school on her back each day, walking about fifteen to twenty minutes like that. What a mama champion she is!

Dorcas wants a business of her own too, but a shop requires three months rent up front plus supplies. She has dreams of her own career but feels torn raising kids and handling domestic things so Jose can realize his career dreams. Sounded very familiar, not unlike what many American couples must balance.

They were a wonderful couple and family to get to know. In addition to running Badilika, Jose is building a career in music and showed me one of his videos. From his reports, this does not sound any easier in Africa than it does in America. Yet he has obvious talent, great determination, and a giant personality, which is a plus.

They were fun to visit and gracious hosts. Jose talked to me about my divorce, praised the strength of women in general, and acknowledged he recognized me as a strong and confident leader just by how I entered a room.

He also felt I could be intimidating to men who may be attracted to me. I couldn't believe this young man from Kenya indicated this, especially when I felt I had shown up very humble, laid back, just "the gal from the Midwest" in Africa. It was surprising, but amazingly similar to feedback I have heard in America from some. (I nearly cried.)

Then he talked about men who marry a second, third, or fourth time, and how they say in Africa, "Once we cry, we always want our first wife." Whew! I didn't expect my divorce, personality, or love life to be a topic at all on this trip, and yet it came up every day in some form or another with the African people.

Later, we walked through the very poor town of Maai Mahiu with our Badilika friends and were introduced to more local people along the way. They helped us understand that because of Maai Mahiu's location between the larger cities of Nairobi and Nakuru, this community began as a sleeping spot for truck drivers. Therefore, hotel options and prostitution became viable businesses. Over the past fifteen years, the town has grown to a population of about eighteen thousand. Unfortunately, drug and sex trafficking are major problems.

We shopped at a store with everything from bottled water to animal figurines to bracelets to home decor. I picked three gifts and one thing for myself, but the bartering began way too high and the guy would not come down to the money I had to spend, so I ended up with only two gifts. I missed shopping where the price was clear and non-negotiable.

I realized how very uncomfortable I was bartering and how I worried about everyone affected. Still, I saved lots of money to buy from the poorest of the poor who have shops (or not) and to donate to the next church we visited.

We went on for tea at a little restaurant down the road, just got served, then our ride came. Oh well. We said goodbye to our friends and proceeded onto the next chapter of the day.

Maai Mahiu is quite new, but very poor and covered in trash. A local man told me there were workers paid to pick up trash but they don't and yet still get paid! I also heard there is no system to get rid of it when it is picked up, so the problems are layered, like all problems in Africa. I saw someone open a water bottle and throw the outside packaging on the ground right in front of me, just as if the earth was the trash can. I was shocked.

Recycling? No such thing here, which really bothered me. I actually contemplated putting at least all our water bottles in a suitcase to recycle at home. (Absurd, I know.)

On the drive back to camp, Nyakio got pulled over by police not knowing why. He accused her of being in a non-passing zone while passing other cars. However, he did not stop the trucks (driven by males) who had done the very same thing at the same time she did.

She had to get out of the car, go to his car, and pay a fine. We were delayed quite awhile with all of this and worried about her when we could not see her anymore. When she returned to the car, she explained the police most likely picked her because she had her own vehicle (a sign of wealth) and she had a car full of *mzungas* (white people) which was another indication of wealth.

This was all very ironic to us, as we had just spent much of the day in Maai Mahiu where we learned prostitution and drug trafficking are major issues. I had asked our friends there where the police were, and they said they do not monitor these activities. Instead, they were out on the highway in groups ticketing drivers for nonexistent violations. Frustrating.

We learned a lot about the culture and their mentality today. Nyakio spoke of the sense of entitlement of some people in Kenya. Plus, she said they know how to coerce Americans to give them handouts so they don't have to do anything. She talked about the fine line between helping people and enabling them. Everything is about balance, even this.

Back at camp, Debbie and I unwound a bit from our day, then met with Jennifer and Sandy to put finishing touches on the women's conferences which were starting the next day. Jennifer, a nurse, would be teaching preventative health over the life span. Sandy, a nutritionist, would provide guidance regarding the relationship between the food we eat and the stages of life we are experiencing.

Debbie, a business consultant, would be sharing ways for the women to utilize their current skill sets to create marketable businesses to support their families. I would be speaking primarily about self-care, self-empowerment, while exploring the differences between healthy and abusive relationships. Our goal was to promote wholistic health, encouraging the women of Kenya to expect more out of life by becoming stronger leaders in their own lives and even greater role models for future generations. Several such women's conferences were scheduled for the week.

After we solidified plans with Jennifer and Sandy, Debbie and I returned to our tent and bounced ideas off each other regarding our specific parts of the seminars and revised our notes. We both just wanted to help so very much. Although we have tons of experience, education, and confidence in our abilities, our audience was extremely different this time and the problems to address far more complex than any we had ever dealt with in the past.

Then we walked down to the lake and took more pictures. This is such a lovely setting — big hills surrounding the still lake, many dormant trees sticking up out of the water, birds of all kinds flying around and all the acacia trees, flowers, and greenery circling it all. Breathtaking!

Dinner was colorful, delicious, and satisfying, the company fantastic. We shared the events of our day together.

As had become our routine, we held our nightly organizational meeting immediately following dinner, then sorted everything we brought over for the women, teachers, school kids, orphans, etc., and divided them appropriately to get to their designated places.

Apparently getting toothbrushes, mosquito nets, pens, books, and any kind of clothing was a big deal.

We closed with prayer and parted to our tents for respite. Debbie and I were both blessed with hot showers, and I exercised my hand, wrist, elbow, and shoulder. As became our habit, we both laid in bed and journaled about the day.

Much to my disappointment, there was still no cell service or wifi. I hadn't communicated with the kids beyond our "the travels went safely" text messages while in the Nairobi airport four days before.

Laura flew to New York City yesterday and started her internship today at Scholastic. I hoped she was happy and adjusting well. I hoped Justin and Pebble were bonding, and everything else was fine back home. Not being able to communicate regularly with them was way out of my comfort zone.

The best I could do was trust all was well and hoped they understood the lack of communication and weren't concerned. I couldn't focus on it too much or I would have gotten very upset.

Africa's beauty was as intense as its layers and layers of problems. The problems could overwhelm me and feel impossible, but I was determined to make a difference with people here, even if it was only by lifting them up while in their presence.

It's only Monday.

Tomorrow is another day, and who knows what it will bring?

Goodnight, Africa.

Day 6

The days started to run together. At home, we heard it was very hot (103 degrees), while here it was rainy and chilly, the tail end of winter, less than sixty degrees.

I woke to African music blasting at 5:30 a.m. I figured out later it was probably how the cooks got started with joy and energy in the kitchen. I couldn't get back to sleep. I listened to the music along with all the animals singing their morning songs.

Debbie and I were prompt for our departure time, and again there were always reasons the group left later than planned. Remaining patient with a relaxed attitude was very important.

We arrived at the church in Gil Gil where we were conducting our first women's conference. The terrain was horribly rough — dirt, rocks, and potholes that would trip a dinosaur!

The organizers greeted us and helped us get settled in. No women had arrived. Around 10:00 a.m., when we were supposed to start, just a few had shown up. The organizers took us (only the presenters) aside for tea, bananas and pastries called *mandozi*. Delicious. Once again, the hospitality was amazing. Out of respect for the people's generosity and the cultural tradition of hospitality, it was very important to receive their offerings graciously.

I needed a restroom. Oh dear. I was led behind a tin door to a short dirt path to a tin outhouse that had a hole in the ground with two cinder blocks beside the hole to squat on. At least there was toilet paper. There were chickens right outside the door. It smelled.

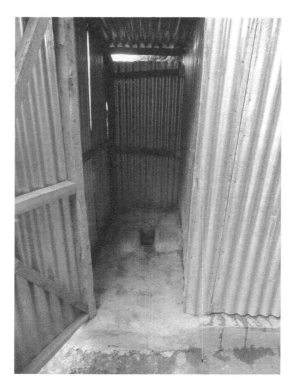

I tried but couldn't go. I was so scared I would fall over in the dirt and other "stuff." I was not very coordinated holding up my skirt and bending my knees so far down. Besides the physical discomfort, I realized I had some psychological barrier to doing this that Freud would probably have been thrilled to analyze. I didn't even understand all the reasons, and I was certainly not a princess, but I just couldn't go. (How do they do it?)

At last we had a full congregation of women. We began seventy-five minutes late. We did well, provided lots of practical information about physical health, nutrition, emotional well-being, and building dreams. The participants seemed engaged and interested in what we had to share. They took notes and asked good questions.

This was my first experience working with an interpreter, and I was amazed at her ability to not only translate my words but also the context and emotion in which I shared them. However, it was also another practice of patience, because I had to say a line or two, then pause for her to repeat it in Swahili, over and over throughout the entire workshop. All of our interpreters throughout the week amazed me. They worked so hard, concentrated so deeply, and translated with such expression. I truly admired them. (Although, technically, I had no idea what they told the women I had said!)

We ran out of time before we had given all our information. The women sang a lively, joy-filled song with abandon when we began and another when we ended, then added an English version so we could sing along.

Then we handed out participation gifts: mosquito nets and toothbrushes. I was asked to give each person a toothbrush. As I went from woman to woman, I started to notice the looks in their tearful eyes, the warm smiles of relief, and the deep appreciation on their faces. They were thrilled! I felt I had handed them gold. This was a bit confusing to me, actually.

Then they served lunch which was colorful, healthy, and delicious. Women came up to us and expressed appreciation and asked if we could stay longer next time. Some said they loved us. Many blessed us.

One woman worked in a mental health unit of a hospital. All of the psychiatric care is paid for by private foundations. People can stay indefinitely inpatient as needed. As a licensed professional counselor, I cannot count how many times I wish that had been possible in America! In that moment, I realized our nation could benefit from the wisdom of this country's practices in some ways, not just the other way around.

I felt good about what we did but at the same time sorry I couldn't meet and know each woman personally. Everyone has a story, and I could only guess what each one had been through. I hoped we made a difference.

When we got into the car afterwards I asked, "What's the big deal with the toothbrushes?" Because this was my first women's conference, I really didn't understand everything yet, especially the participants' emotional reactions to receiving one toothbrush.

Seasoned team members explained to me that toothbrushes are considered a luxury in rural Kenya. People do not have access to them, nor could they likely afford them if they could travel to where they are available. They told me each woman would likely go home and share that toothbrush with all the members of her family until it fell apart. Usually, cleaning their teeth (if they do anything at all) involves chewing on the bark of a certain tree with qualities that are supposed to help with dental hygiene.

All my life, I have never known the value of a toothbrush. I was speechless.

We got on our way. The pouring rain had stopped but left rivers of water and muddy terrain to travel through.

As part of our efforts to improve life for the Kenyan people, we needed to plant eight trees in upcoming visits, so we had to take a side trip on the way back to camp to buy them. I thought my bladder was going to burst but didn't have the courage to ask to stop or go behind a tree or anything. I just tried to distract myself.

After forty-five minutes at the nursery, finally we were on our way. A beautiful double rainbow greeted us after another bit of rain. That, along with the sun peaking through across the valley, was like a painting from God Himself.

Africa is just so beautiful! We also saw some zebras really close up at a corner off the highway. Their stripes were so striking. We were taught they are like snowflakes, no two just alike, which is hard to believe but also very cool.

Sightings of goats and mules occur all the time too. Oh, and the gas station stop! Long — nothing was quick in Africa. Although full service was the norm, the workers were very slow and required constant correction. Gas, air in the tires, and cleaning windows took more than one request and at least three servicemen. Nyakio asked us to watch the pump and be sure they cleared it to zero before starting because sometimes they don't so they can make more money.

Gas prices were eighty-three shillings per liter, four liters equalled a gallon, so the cost was $3.32 per gallon, approximately.

The driving continued to be crazy. People passed without proper time, created lanes where there were none, and really didn't seem too concerned about the presence of other vehicles. It was unreal!

Finally at 6:00 p.m. we arrived back at camp. I was tired, having drifted off slightly the last twenty minutes or so, and I was more than ready for a bathroom. I think I urinated more than I ever had in my life at one time before. What a relief!

I sat for tea with John in the lodge. We shared the stories of the day and relaxed together. I liked this spontaneous time with him.

Through his generous insistence, I borrowed his prepaid African cell phone to leave messages with both Laura and Justin, as my international phone plan turned out to be worthless, as we were just too far from any cell tower. We still had not had any luck getting the wifi fixed at the camp either. The kids and I had been out of touch with each other longer than ever before in their lives, but at least they knew I arrived in Africa okay, and I knew they arrived home from Colorado okay.

I was relieved to think that when they checked their messages later that day, they would understand I was fine, but there was simply no cell service or wifi available. I missed them, and Pebble, too.

Dinner was delicious again, but our group had to eat outside which was uncomfortable. The weather was still rainy and chilly.

We had another meeting briefly sharing our reflections from the day's experiences and doing group readings from the Episcopal Church tradition. This is called *compline* or "the last prayer of the day."

Tomorrow we have to leave at 7:30 in the morning to go to Nakuru for another women's conference. We'll see how it compares to today.

We've seen mosquitos now and killed some. We wore bug spray all day and evening and took our malaria pills daily. Our beds had mosquito nets to protect us. So far, everyone appeared healthy. Some were a bit sleep deprived though, and every day required everyone to be patient because of the endless list of distractions, unexpected logistical issues, or whatever!

The good Lord knew I could always benefit from another experience requiring patience, so here I was given the opportunity again.

Goodnight, Africa.

Day 7

Despite having slept fine, my morning began with explosive diarrhea. (Sorry, but it's true.) The toilets didn't have enough water in them to clean the sides with each flush, so I washed it myself with toilet paper so my tent-mate wouldn't have to tolerate that disgusting sight. Anyway, I got ready for the day, didn't really feel sick, but kept going to the bathroom every ten minutes or so.

Our team nurse gave me antidiarrheal medicine which helped but the thought of a ten hour day on rough, muddy rural roads, and a "bathroom" that's only a hole in the ground to squat over, just sounded unnerving, so I reluctantly stayed back and rested.

I felt bad "abandoning" the team, but of course, they embraced me and my decision, reminding me that I gave a talk just the day before empowering women to make self-care a bigger priority in their lives. (I'm so stubborn!)

So as the team departed without me, I headed back to our tent, and on the way one of the staff members stopped, looked at me puzzled saying, "You rest today?" I said, "Yes," indicating I wasn't in great shape. He said, "Can I get you a hot water bottle?" (So thoughtful and sweet.) I said, "Oh, yes, *Asante* (thank you)!" Everyone was so kind there.

As I walked along the path toward our tent, all of a sudden I realized a whole group of monkeys were playing and climbing all over Sandy and Jennifer's tent! Adorable! I stopped and watched, took pictures and made a short video. What a blessing! Thank you, God, for this little light in my day.

I went to the tent after my monkey fix, got changed into comfy sweats, and once my water bottle arrived (my favorite new companion), I crawled into bed with the chills, but fell asleep quickly, waking only briefly to urinate and stayed there until the afternoon. Wow, I had never done that before!

Rising at 1:30 p.m., I got cozy in the chair and spent the afternoon reading a book I had packed which fed me spiritually, watched the monkeys play out the window, drank water, and ate a small cracker every half hour.

I felt so much better after sleeping. The fever broke, and everything settled.

Ironically, many of the topics in the book related to disease, healing, mind over matter, emotions, and the body. Interesting timing, huh?

Finally everyone returned, and they reported they'd had a long but productive day. The women's conference was well attended with good responses to the material.

Barely eating any dinner, I decided to play it safe — a little rice, a roll, and a cup of tea. All felt good going down. As a new traveling team member, I had been coached before we left about some things to remember about the food and water in Africa.

First and foremost, under no circumstances were we to drink the water, not even to brush our teeth. The African people have built an immunity to it, but Americans with our filtered, treated water at home cannot handle the water there. So we literally drank and brushed our teeth out of bottled water the whole time.

As far as food was concerned, we were told to be careful with any leafy greens, salads, and fruits that were not peeled. Some suggested we be very choosy about meat. I had barely eaten any meat and followed all the instructions given. The food I ate always looked and tasted very inviting. Some say everyone has some kind of reaction on their first trip, so I guess the differences just got to my system a bit. No big deal.

Loved the fellowship at dinner. Our team was so kind and loving. Word apparently got around what I had dealt with that day, and everyone checked in with me. With so much compassion coming from the group, I felt like I had a family around me while being halfway around the world from home.

After dinner, we had our Team Meeting and compline. We read scripture aloud together, prayed, planned the next day's transportation schedule, and shared reflections of the day.

Fran, our chaplain, asked us to try to apply our sharing to the scripture that had been read. Tonight's Bible scripture was about the workers in the vineyard in Matthew, who all worked different amounts of hours but the owner paid them all the same and said it was his choice what to do with his resources. This displeased some of the employees who had worked longer shifts, of course.

So I said, "You all went out and worked in the field today, I stayed back and rested, but we all got paid the same — nothing!" The group had a good laugh over that, but then I got serious and thanked them all for their support and kindness as I felt it all day long.

People had some big-time testimonies tonight. My favorite, though, was John's. He was at the Ngeya Primary School just to catch his ride, but at the same time the big cooking pot broke (cracked) and was deemed unrepairable. A cooking pot costs fifty-thousand shillings, and the head mistress anticipated it would probably take at least two months to come up with enough donations from parents as this was a very poor region.

There wasn't any government money left for the school this year either. Therefore, she would have to lay off the two cooks whose families would now likely starve, and no school lunch would be available to the two thousand students for two months, so they might also starve. The one cup of rice, beans, or maize they received at school was quite possibly the only meal many of them would eat in a day.

But guess what? John's congregation from home had given him one-thousand dollars to use at his discretion as long as it went for the needs of children. So he was able, literally, to reach in his wallet and spontaneously hand over fifty-thousand shillings (five hundred U.S. dollars) to school officials, and they were able to arrange for the new pot to be bought and delivered within the next day or two!

The cooks cried, everyone was so grateful, and John felt like he was blessed to be part of a miracle. God is GREAT! These experiences were so amazing, heart-warming, and encouraging to hear.

I was also so thankful to be healthy in a warm bed again that night, having showered extra long and shaved for the first time in a week. My "Traveler's Diarrhea," as it is called, was easily managed and short-lived. Like all things in Africa, the days were a bit unpredictable, but we seemed to be making a difference with what we were doing, and that was what made it all worth it.

So another day came to a close in Africa. We'd been gone from home a week now and would return in a week. We only had three more days "out in the field" doing projects, then the Safari, the Hippo Tour, and travel days left. I knew it would all go quickly, but the blessings and memories would last a lifetime. I felt grateful beyond belief.

Goodnight, Africa.

Day 8

For me, the day began with a breakfast of hot tea and a roll. I was still being conservative about food and probably would remain that way the rest of the trip, just to be safe. After we ate, before we left, the monkeys came along and tried to get food out of the dining area. They were so cute, funny, and fast.

Called velvet monkeys, they were all ages and sizes. A mama even carried one under her belly. They swung through the trees, paraded along the sidewalk, and jumped on the roof. The workers explained they were considered rodents here, like our rats. How could something so cute be a rodent?

Then off we went to Nyakio's mother's house in the Naivasha area. Nyakio's father left their family, so "Mama Nyakio" raised her three children on her own. (In Africa, mothers are called "Mama" with their oldest child's name, so there, I would be referred to as "Mama Laura.") Anyway, Mama Nyakio became a wise business woman despite her challenges and now owns a large home, land, and has staff of her own, all symbols of wealth and success in Africa.

We walked a bit around her land and then were shown the latest excitement — a very tiny building erected on her land to house the required machines to make sanitary napkins, a one room factory full of promise and hope!

Nyakio gave us a demonstration on how sanitary napkins were made. The goal was to completely supply the women of Agatha Amani House, sell them at a lower price in the local market and eventually distribute widely. The main ingredient, fluffy pulp, was not readily available then, but they were working on it. Nine hundred could be made in a day at full capacity.

Girls in Africa often stop going to school when they menstruate because sanitary napkins are not readily available, and they aren't prepared or informed about it in the first place. This creates a whole layer of problems — uneducated girls, often becoming wives and mothers very early in life or being sold in the sex trade.

The hope was to increase education about menstruation and the accessibility of the products so girls will stay in school, get a solid education, and hold off on marriage and parenthood until much later. Who would have ever known the lack of sanitary napkins could actually be a factor in girls being uneducated and at risk for the sex trade or very early marriage and motherhood?

Our next stop was Agatha Amani House which is outside of Naivasha, extremely secluded, on a very muddy, rough terrain road.

Nyakio's dream was to create a shelter for women and children who needed safe haven from gender-based violence. Her mother (named "Agatha," aka Mama Nyakio) donated the land for it. Thus, the name "Agatha *Amani* (meaning "peace") House."

Nyakio gave us a tour through the crops, gardens, animals, and home. This was after we were introduced to all the girls, staff, and their babies. They sang for us, and we all prayed together.

Eventually they served tea and pastries. I was asked to give them a speech of empowerment while we ate and fellowshipped together. I had not rehearsed this but spoke from my heart whatever came.

Mainly, I reminded them they are beloved children of God, they have a right to be happy, and they are not their circumstances. I expressed the importance of loving themselves, letting go of problems, changing their thoughts that cause undo suffering, and believing they can take control of their lives and their futures.

Afterwards, the girls expressed thanks for this encouragement and seemed to have new ways to consider looking at life. They asked if I could just stay there with them. (So sweet.)

One girl admitted she was considering running away from the house that day and going off to Mombasa which is clear on the East coast of Kenya, but now she was reconsidering. She had a one-year-old little girl she would've been dragging along, too! Mombasa was many hours drive away, and they would have been alone walking. Imagine the dangers they could have encountered on such a trip!

I felt lucky to have been able to share this time with everyone at Agatha Amani House. They were so appreciative. Mama Nyakio publicly thanked me as well and reiterated some of my message to them.

I was very impressed with all the self-sustaining practices utilized there. In just four years, they have accomplished a great deal.

We left, ate our boxed lunches in the van, and headed to Maai Mahiu to the Ngeya Primary School for our day of celebration with them.

We arrived, and the children surrounded our van. They liked to shake hands, high five, and touch my hair. I could hardly get around them to go to the common area outside for the ceremony. (I felt like Elvis!)

Two thousand children, twenty-six teachers, and eleven additional staff awaited our arrival. The children wore tattered uniforms and shoes, some clearly the wrong size, and all very dirty, especially since the rain had been quite steady, and the ground was so muddy. I wondered how often they got to wash their uniforms let alone their bodies.

In Africa, we were treated like celebrities, always entertained, prayed for, and shown tremendous gratitude. Today was no exception. The children sang songs, recited poetry with great passion, and said a beautiful prayer.

The head mistress announced to the children how the big cooking pot broke the previous day, but God had provided a new one through K2K's John Bishop, so they could still eat at school and not be deprived of that for a couple of months while donations were collected.

The two thousand children roared, squealed, jumped up and down, and clapped with gratitude. I've never seen or heard anything like this response before! If I had anticipated the reaction that was coming, I would have videotaped it on my phone. Unforgettable! (At the same time, I was actually embarrassed at how American children take so much for granted, as we adults do as well.)

What a wonderful moment to witness! And I was so happy for John, because he made it happen.

We were given the privilege of passing out gifts, medals, trophies, and certificates as awards for academics, behavior, leadership, and athletics. I got to give out the "Most Improved" Boy and Girl a booklet and K2K medals around their necks. Rebecca and Leonard were there names.

After much celebration, dancing, and clapping, we were given tours of their classrooms. They were so proud to show us, even though the dirt floors, broken windows, and lack of desks were very obvious. Very enlightening for me to witness well-disciplined children who outwardly showed appreciation and respect for their teachers and gave God glory for the opportunity to learn. Again, my mind wandered back to the American school system and students' boredom, misconduct, and general disrespect for the institution. How have we failed our kids so?

God was very much a part of public school here. The teachers and students freely prayed with each other and gave thanks to God for anything and everything they received.

When James asked us how American schools were different, we told him that God was not allowed in our public schools, and he was dumbfounded! This made no sense to him at all, even when we explained how America was full of many religions, and one could no longer be represented in schools over the others.

What would Africa do if they did not have this kind of openness and relationship with God? I cannot fathom it.

Soon it was time to say goodbye to the children. Again, they surrounded me so intensely, I could hardly walk. They did not want to let me go and grabbed my arms tightly. I felt like a celebrity. More handshakes, high fives, and lots of bye-byes later, I pulled myself away from them. I suppose they don't cross paths with Americans too often.

Next we met with all the staff in the meeting room and again were thanked. We gave them each a pack of four pens which you would think was gold. They actually ripped open the packages and started sharing all the pens, not realizing we had brought an entire pack for each of them. They were flabbergasted they got to keep all four pens to themselves!

They were gracious and hospitable, sharing pop and muffins with us. It was a nice way to round out the experience.

After final hugs and well wishes, we headed back to camp. Another member of our team got Traveler's Diarrhea, and many were just tired, but the rewards of the day were incredible.

Dinner was delicious. I avoided all the yummy looking African dishes with veggies and spices and meats and just had potatoes, rice, and rolls. I felt so good, I didn't want to take any chances. I was so tempted to have some of the chocolate cake, but I only took one bite of someone else's, and it was delicious. I just didn't want to miss any other experiences we had in store.

The fellowship at dinner was delightful as always, and we had a shortened devotion tonight. Several people blessed me with compliments about my short talk today at Agatha Amani House, and I was really moved by my peers' support.

The K2K Community Team was an exceptional group of people to work with. They are generous in spirit, service, and resources. Life will be different from now on for me because of this experience.

Goodnight, Africa.

Day 9

I struggled to get out of bed this morning even though I slept well. I had several short dreams that I remember, but none really made sense. I suppose I could have looked for the metaphor, but I needed to hurry to get ready.

The monkeys entertained us at breakfast again which was so much fun! I doubt I would ever tire of them.

Then off we went with a van load with several stops to make. My first responsibility was a women's conference at the Osborne Library in Maai Mahiu. We started over two hours late, and I found myself being very impatient. However, someone explained to me most of these women probably had to get the children off to school, perhaps feed the chickens, and then may have walked several miles to attend. Immediately, I felt more patient with this additional information. So part of it was the pace of this country, part of it was the realities mentioned, and part of it was leaders insisting we wait for all who said they were coming. Sixty-five out of one-hundred showed up.

Finally we got started. I gave my self-care/empowerment talk as usual and spontaneously decided to share a bit about my divorce. The women seemed responsive to it, even though we acknowledged it's much tougher in Africa than America, generally speaking.

They asked some difficult questions regarding their own circumstances, and I felt the frustration of not being able to thoroughly address their concerns in the few moments I had for each one.

Then I moved on to Badilika to help with a conference for women who are married to alcoholics or have some other close male who is an addict. I gave my self-care/empowerment talk with an Al-Anon twist to it. We talked at length about the Serenity Prayer, being a leader in your home and in your life, and not enabling anyone.

The problems were layered and complicated. Sometimes I felt inadequate blowing into a town giving them a slice of advice only to scurry out to the next town without thoroughly working through issues near and dear to their hearts. However, we did what we could with the best of intentions.

As we were exiting Badilika, along walked school children from the previous day heading home. They saw me, recognized me, and some came running to say hello again, get a high five or a hug. Their faces lit up like a Christmas tree, as did mine.

However, I was also a bit haunted by this sight. I realized I was watching children of all ages walking across this town, thick with drug traffic and prostitution. We had made agreements as a team that none of us would walk alone across this town for safety reasons, and yet these small children were doing this every day. It wouldn't take much of anything to lure these children to the back of a shop and do anything they want to with them. What a disturbing, frightening thought.

I returned to the women's conference at the church and things were still going on. When presentations were done, we passed out toothbrushes and mosquito nets, big treasures to all.

Then we were done, but other team members had work to complete there, so Debbie and I went out and spent time with the children who were about, some of whom we had met at church last Sunday.

We played games and sang songs with them. They sang for us too and shared poetry. They wanted lots of affection, hand holding, hugs, and to touch my hair, of course.

I thought this was the very best use of my time. Hopefully, the children felt loved. One (Susan) asked if I had any crackers. I had one protein bar in my bag, not nearly enough for all, so I said, "No." I figured she must be hungry.

She pointed out her nearby house, and said she thinks it's cute. She also let me meet her puppy, Tommy. Very adorable. I secretly wondered, how does a family feed a puppy enough when they sometimes can't feed their own children?

A couple of boys started throwing rocks at mules, and I asked them to stop. I talked to the children about the importance of being kind to each other and to all animals. I doubt they've heard that before, and I'm not sure what all they understood, but I know they knew I didn't like it.

Before we left, I spent a few moments with Susan, my hands firmly on her shoulders, bent down looking straight in her eyes, and reiterated things we had talked about before. I figured this would be my last chance to speak with her, and I wanted her to hear me encourage her to stay in school, keep reading, and not let anyone or anything keep her from fulfilling her dreams.

Looking deeply into my eyes, I felt strongly she was listening, and I secretly hoped she would never, ever in her whole life through forget this moment, my genuine love and care for her, and the profound life messages I was attempting to share. Then what words came out of her mouth?

"Next time you come, bring crackers."

Did she hear me at all? I'll never really know. Her request reminded me that our basic physical needs must be met before we can move on to other, less tangible needs. If she's hungry, how could she ever concentrate in school, for example, let alone leave everything behind she has ever known to go to a far off university somewhere?

Regardless, we had to go, and as we left, the children held on very tightly, desperate for us to stay. They hung around the van until the last possible moment. It was hard to leave them behind knowing the tough realities they face and will continue to face. I hoped they would remember our kindnesses to them and our messages to stay in school as long as possible and hold on firmly to their dreams.

Back in the van, which was overloaded with people, another workday was done. As we drove out of town, more children recognized us in the van and waved excitedly. Will they always remember the day the Americans came?

Dinner was outside again, and we found ourselves cold. I didn't bring a coat with me to Africa at all, thinking my sweats and my thinnest hoodie would be warm enough. Everyone reported this was an unusually chilly, rainy June.

I chose to eat a bit more today, and the body did not rebel. I was so very thankful. I do like many of the African dishes but just didn't want to be ill and miss anything.

Tonight during compline we were treated to videos Bob had put together of our week which included some of my talk at the Agatha Amani House.

We were also given the opportunity to share our reflections from the last day or two. I loved hearing everyone's stories. There is so much going on in our little group, blessings we gave and in turn received.

My life truly will never be the same again.

Goodnight, Africa.

Day 10

We actually got to sleep in a little more today, not having to leave until 9:00 a.m. This was helpful, especially since it was our last day of conferences. However, the monkeys were not around this morning, so I wondered if we were too late for them.

I asked the staff where the monkeys were, and they jokingly said, "Saturday is their day off." Laughter is a universal language. They were such a delightful, kind, thoughtful staff.

So we got on our way and headed to the Anglican Church of Kenya All Saints Hall in Naivasha, a town of about 350,000 people. It was bustling as one would expect in a city this size.

The compound was very scenic and well-cared for. There was a smaller, older stone church, and a newer, bigger one, plus several outer buildings with various purposes. I took quite a few pictures as the surrounding views were incredible as well.

We held two conferences there, and I was involved in both. One was another women's conference like we had done all week, and the other was for executive directors and staff of nonprofit social service agencies. The purpose was to help them begin to dialogue more with one another, build a stronger community network and increase collaboration. Apparently this was a problem, with competition between them being the norm.

I was privileged to get to talk to this group as well, focusing on Scarcity vs. Abundance Mentality, changing their thoughts, the power of the mind, self-care, teamwork, etc. Incorporating some exercises from my Jack Canfield trainings that prove the power of our thoughts, I appeared to capture their attention and amaze them!

Again, the conferences started extremely late. I still had not adjusted to "Africa Time," meaning the pace, not the time zone. As Americans, we are probably too stressed about time, the concern of starting or arriving late always on our minds, people speeding to get to where they are supposed to be, others leaving if someone doesn't arrive promptly. Yet in Africa, I felt like there was little awareness of time at all. I could be wrong. Living somewhere in the middle of these two extremes might be the best balance of all.

Despite the time issue, the African people we have encountered at our conferences this week were so appreciative. They all wanted more time with us, ironically. We jammed everything we could (I think) into this week and gave away hundreds of toothbrushes and mosquito nets, tons of information, and lots of love.

The goodbyes began today because we won't be with the shelter staff or the interns anymore. I admit they were not easy to part from. The participants want us to come back and stay longer also. They wished us God's blessings for a safe journey. They expressed love and appreciation for us. They asked us to remember them, and I promised them I would. The connection was profound.

On we went back down the road. We took Mama Nyakio back to her home and said our goodbyes. She seemed surprised we were only staying two weeks. Perspectives were just so different there.

Fortunately, we were able to stop and shop just a bit at the cool little store right outside Camp Crescent. It was called "The Farm Shop," and some of the others had enjoyed it earlier in the week and suggested we make an effort to go there. I was thrilled to see price tags and enjoyed not having to barter. I bought a basket with lid made of beads for a friend, a little purse for Laura, and homemade applesauce for Justin. I missed connecting with the kids. I wondered again how everything was going for them.

Earlier that week I purchased several gifts from women whose "stores" were merely blankets on the ground with homemade products spread across them. Because I admired their craftiness and wanted to show support for their courage in creating a business, I spent the majority of my money shopping from them. The jewelry and baskets were all colorful and good quality. What fun to support these women in this way!

A fun little outing, "The Farm Shop" symbolized the beginning of our free time and play for the remaining days here. Tonight we packed up as we had to move out of Crescent Camp for just one night to go on safari, and then we returned for the last night.

Dinner was nice — more great fellowship — then on to our meeting to close the day.

I shared the exercises with the team I had done at the conference, so they could know them and enjoy them. We shared reflections as a group as always then did the nightly devotions.

We shared extra prayers too. This reminded me of my church upbringing more than anything we've done in a formal or informal way religiously speaking since coming here.

It seemed everyone felt good about what we've done, even though so much remains to be changed. We've done well, each person bringing such valuable gifts to the work. Everyone contributed significantly.

Now, hopefully we can all enjoy some fellowship and delight in the beautiful African scenery and wildlife these next couple of days before heading back to America, a place that feels emotionally and physically very, very far away.

Life will be different upon my return, I just know it.

Goodnight, Africa.

Day 11

Early to rise today, as we had a two hour drive to church in Nakuru. We also had to pack a backpack for overnight and pack our suitcases to be locked up while we were gone, as we return tomorrow night for our last night in Africa. No monkeys again this morning, but breakfast was pleasant, and we got on our way.

The drive to church was like a pre-safari wildlife show. We saw zebras, gazelles, a baboon walking along the highway, the first horses we've seen, along with the usual cows, goats, and mules. We also had a beautiful view of the Great Rift Valley, the hills, and Lake Elementaita. The trip went really quickly with so much entertainment along the way.

Debbie and I spent the drive asking the rest of the team questions about different aspects of life in Africa we had not yet learned about.

For example, families used to display their dead loved ones at home for several days, but the health department put a stop to that due to the ebola crisis. Many families still prefer (and can only afford) to bury their loved ones on their own land with simple markers. Those with more means may hire a funeral home.

There are ambulances in larger communities. When people stay in the hospital, if they need to eat, the families have to bring in food. Much of women and children's health care is paid for through private funding, but sometimes costs remain. If someone dies in the hospital, their body will not be released to the family until the bill is paid.

There are three types of marriage ceremonies. One is a verbal agreement between two people, another is a civil ceremony, and the other is a religious ceremony. Ceremony choice is sometimes financially based. What kind of union you choose can also affect property issues. Men are in charge of all decisions regarding frequency of sex, how many children they will have, and who will care for them.

The Maasi tribe still has arranged marriages. When a baby girl is born, her spouse has been chosen and paid for. In all likelihood, he is much, much older than her. We did not visit the Maasi community nearby on this particular trip, but team members explained they have in the past, but they are a very private, secluded people.

When a husband dies in Africa, his family of origin can take control of the property and finances, and depending on how they feel about his wife or what kind of relationship they perceived they had, may include her and care for her, or they may throw her out with nothing. They can also take the children. All of this can happen with divorce as well.

There are legal services and laws to protect the rights of women and children, but they are not enforced well, especially in the more rural villages. Some in powerful positions can be bribed to delay a case or make it such an impossible, drawn out process that a woman can't last it financially or emotionally. It's really shocking.

Although supposedly only one marriage at a time is legal here, cultural tradition wins out sometimes. Men can bring in a second wife, unannounced, and the first wife then has a choice to make. She can either become the housekeeper and cook for them, losing her position as the main wife, or she can choose to leave, but then would likely be left with nothing, sometimes not even her children. What kind of options are those? Apparently, these sad realities are improving with each generation, but we've certainly learned a lot about this directly from locals experiencing it in one form or another.

After our lively question and answer session in the van, we arrived at church, St. Christopher's in Nakuru, and at last the sun was shining brightly, and it was dry. It's the first day I haven't felt cold since arriving. The K2K medical team arrived as well, and this was the one time for all of us to be together, so we took team photos out on the church lawn and got to know each other a bit.

The church compound was just beautiful — lots of flowers, an old stone church, and several outer buildings with various purposes. They called themselves a "family" church that "lives thanksgiving." They have five services each Sunday. This was the English speaking one, and it was a lovely two and a half hour service. The music was powerful and quite contemporary. I knew most of the songs and could easily sing along.

The Bishop Dean Wolfe from Kansas gave the sermon and did a very nice job. The pastor spent significant time acknowledging our group, and the congregation showed tremendous gratitude for our work and presence.

This congregation's members seemed more worldly, educated and financially viable than the church members we met in more rural areas. The people here appeared to have more resources than any group we had seen thus far.

After church, we had tea and visited with people. Once again, we were treated with such generous hospitality.

At this point, two of our team members had to go elsewhere, so we had our first goodbyes with each other. Of course, I cried telling them "so long." My emotions triggered so profoundly I think because I knew our separation from them was the first indication that our experience was nearing its end. Plus, the work we did had been charged, emotional, and draining.

With today's goodbyes complete, we headed out and went to the Lake Nakuru National Park and ate our boxed lunches while our leader purchased our safari tickets. The landscape was just breathtaking, and on our way to Lake Nakuru Lodge we saw many animals.

We were greeted at the lodge with warm washcloths to freshen up and small glasses of juice. Refreshing! We checked into our lovely rooms and out our back door and small deck were several baboons trying to get our attention. Maybe they thought we had food for them. They were hilarious, but we were told not to leave our doors open at any time as they would enter and could be dangerous. I just loved them though.

We got changed. At last I wore my Kansas to Kenya cap and a ponytail. Very relaxing. Soon we were back out on safari, and we saw two kinds of monkeys, baboons, zebras, rhinoceros, gazelles, cape buffalo, water bucks, antelope, four female lions, and several birds.

The weather was absolutely perfect, and we enjoyed standing up in the van and looking out all sides to find the animal treasures. The breeze blew comfortably, and the sun shone, offering our first natural Vitamin C since arriving.

I felt like I was in heaven! This was a whole other aspect of Africa, and it took my breath away. I felt so blessed to be able to have this experience and still could hardly believe it had all been real even though we've been here a week and a half. I AM IN AFRICA!!!

We returned to the lodge, had a little transition time, ate dinner, which was buffet style and full of delicious variety. Having shared another meal of great fellowship with our team, off to our rooms we went for the night.

As I laid in my bed surrounded by the mosquito net, I thought adjusting to life back home might be a bit of a challenge. I'm not sure I will fit in America as well anymore. It was all a lot to absorb and comprehend.

We were in the final stages of the trip now. I reminded myself to just relax and play. Save the concerns of adjustment for later and enjoy this moment. Indeed, I'm one of the luckiest girls I know.

Goodnight, Africa.

Day 12

We rose early to a beautiful day, had a scrumptious breakfast at Lake Nakuru Lodge (one of the prettiest places I've ever seen on Earth and the closest to the Equator I'd ever been), then headed out on safari in high hopes of seeing anything, but especially giraffes.

Nature did not disappoint. The sun was pleasant and inviting, and the animals really gave us a show!

We saw lots and lots of baboons. The babies (I think) were my favorite. They felt a little concerned about us and clutched their mamas closely. The baboons sat on stumps, on rocks or along the road and looked at us like we were nuts. Their back sides were often pink, swollen and quite unsightly really, but we heard this was a status symbol for them. (I'm super glad it's not for us!) Nature is just so fascinating!

We also saw all kinds of birds, so many varieties, shapes, colors, and sizes. So much fun! I can't remember all their names, there were just so many.

Lots of impalas, zebras, gazelles, and cape buffalo were out and about — too many to count, and we got really close to them. Wonderful views. Some animals seemed undeterred by our presence and others seemed anxious and moved away if we stuck around too long.

We came around a turn and there with a beautiful green tree, the lush hills and blue sky all behind it, a tall, majestic giraffe stood. He was chewing and unconcerned about us. I nearly cried, as I was so excited for this! I could have stared at him all day even though he barely moved. Our driver graced us with plenty of time for pictures and videos, as we didn't know if this would be the only giraffe we would see, but eventually we had to keep moving.

Not far down the road we worked our way around a large turn and were overwhelmingly blessed with a group of twelve giraffes all hanging out, some eating, some walking across the road, some standing, some sitting. They were all sizes. Unbelievable moment in my life! I wept in gratitude while at the same time felt melancholy for all the people who will never see this sight. Incredible. Creation is miraculous and difficult to even describe in words, but this was definitely one of the highlights of my life so far.

A little further down the way was a small group of young giraffes with one female adult. Our bus driver called this "kindergarten" and told us one mama stays with the babies while the other moms go off to eat so they can come back and nurse their babies. It's like day care for giraffes — amazing! This reminded me of play dates with our friends' babies in America or childcare swapping I had done with my friends years ago.

The animal kingdom is just so fascinating. We drove on and were spoiled with the beautiful climate, awesome scenery, and all the furry friends around.

Then we came to a waterfall which was cool to see, but I admit I've never seen a waterfall with dirty water before. It had been so rainy and muddy, so I guess that's why.

To get there we crossed a little pathetic bridge that had a warning sign, then barely made it up the hill. The driver, Maina (pronounced "Mina") had to back the van up and make a harder run for it to make it up, but he did it!

We got out of the vans, took lots of pictures, and just enjoyed the scenery together.

On we went, more animals, and on to Baboon Cliffs, a lookout point overseeing Lake Nakuru and the town, off to the side. The water was high, so even a road usually in view down below was completely flooded. Normally, flamingos were sighted here, but due to the flooding, they were unable to eat the algae they needed, so migration was required.

At this spot we were blessed to be in the company of a new creature — a very bright, colorful lizard. He was shiny, bluish-green with a pink/orange head, maybe a foot long with his tail. Very cool!

There was a sign explaining how groups of elephants pick a tree to ram against until all the fruit falls off, and then they enjoy the meal together. However, there aren't any more elephants in this park, as they were smarter and stronger than the fences and too close to town (Nakuru) and caused problems. Therefore, to see elephants on safari in Kenya, you have to go to one quite a ways north and west from here.

On the way to Baboon Cliffs, I noticed a sign that said, "Out of Africa Lookout" 1.3 km which is less than a mile. "Out of Africa" is one of my all-time favorite movies I have loved for thirty years. I asked the driver if we could please go up there, and he said he couldn't take us there. He assured me the view was very much like Baboon Cliffs, but that wasn't the point to me. Oh well, I'm in Africa! *Hakuna Matata* ("No big deal.")

I found out later, the second van in our group got lost and couldn't find Baboon Cliffs, but they did go to the Out of Africa Lookout, so I could see their pictures sometime. I was also a bit disappointed and frustrated to realize while in Nairobi I was just a few miles from the Karen Blixen Museum and only ten to twelve miles from the house used in the film too. There was no extra time for individual touring. I had to trust the fact that if I am meant to see those things, I will one day. I know how very blessed I've been to be here at all!

So, after Baboon Cliffs we headed back to the lodge and still saw animals along the way.

At one point, we came upon a strange sight. A whole group of female impalas were standing together in a line, all facing one direction as still as they could. In the front of them stood a male doing the same. Our driver said they were on high alert and a predator must be near.

We proceeded down the road just a bit and there, sprawled out on a big limb taking a rest was a leopard! So stunning! We couldn't believe our good fortune. He briefly stayed there then got down and disappeared in the tall grasses but his presence was the reason for the "on guard" behavior of the impalas.

I hope they stayed safe from him.

A couple of members of our group have been coming to Africa and on safari for seven years and had never seen a leopard. What a treat! If we would have stopped at the Out of Africa Lookout, we probably would have missed him.

I teared up several times in awe of this experience and the beauty of these animals, taking in the sheer perfection of nature.

We headed back to the lodge to pack up and have lunch, and while we waited we took turns recording our testimony of the trip to be transcribed at some point.

Lunch was incredibly good, and we sat outside looking out over the hills and grasses of the park, blessed with visits from baboons and warthogs.

Then we left, headed back to our home away from home, Camp Crescent at Lake Naivasha. On the way, we made a quick stop at an ATM and while sitting there, men came up to the van windows and tried to sell us stuff.

Many carried cards or postcards and claimed it was their personal artwork. Strangely enough, however, I had seen these same cards ("originals") everywhere! I said, "No."

Felt really good to get back to camp (like coming home in a way) and after a brief break getting checked back in, Debbie and I sat on our front deck enjoying the sun and the view. Before now, we had had little time to just bask in our surroundings and take it all in.

Soon we headed down to the lake for our Hippo Tour. Joseph was our tour guide, and six of us shared the same boat. We wore life jackets and headed out. His safety talk included informing us that hippos are the deadliest animal to humans in Africa, are very territorial, and if they get concerned, will crush the boat. However, they won't eat us because they are herbivores. (How comforting…)

Despite that unsettling truth, I quickly became mesmerized with all the beautiful, unique birds before us. So many with such variety in color, personality, and size!

After that, we headed to "hippo territories" in the water, often between trees, somewhat close to shore. They have designated areas and stay in their "families." They don't like their picture taken, so many go under water completely if they catch on.

The tour guide knows them very well, where their territories are, and how many belong in each family. This made for a great tour and ease in spotting them.

We saw a few different hippos, one or two at a time, but then we managed to find a family of six, all with their heads above water at the same time. What a unique experience watching a hippo family just hanging out in their territory!

Taking lots of pictures and videos, we delighted in the beauty of these animals in their natural environment. I could hardly believe my good fortune when suddenly I realized the one closest to us was staring us down pretty intensely. He wasn't moving, like, at all.

A bit concerned, I turned to Joseph and said, "You see how the one in the front is staring and not looking too thrilled about us being here?" Joseph replied, "Yes, he's the guard and is keeping his eye on us. He's probably not comfortable with us being here this long." So I suggested maybe it was time to move on, but Joseph remained calm and kept the boat in place.

Then, a noise came out of the hippo's mouth I have never heard in my life! A deep, intense bellow roared from his body, and yet he still didn't move an inch. I was like, "What was THAT???" Joseph said that he was giving us a verbal warning now.

At that point, I admit I was nervous and uneasy about our safety. You never want to disrespect nature, ever! We had seen the hippos plenty — definitely not worth losing our lives over. But Joseph remained steadfast, feeling confident everything was fine. Fortunately, the hippo remained in his spot and let us bask in their presence a bit longer.

Soon after, we shifted to an area that was a bit in the distance but cool to see with giraffes, zebras and wildebeests. They were a bit far away to get a really good view, but nonetheless, awesome. That was a part of the park people were allowed to walk through for a fee, as there are no predators there.

We also saw some African gentlemen fishing with a large net. Their non-verbals indicated they weren't too keen on us floating by, but we were so enthralled with them. They caught three to four large carp while we were in their midst and had to work pretty hard to wrestle them in.

I thought to myself ... would these men and their families have eaten tonight if they hadn't made a catch? Scary thought. It's not the first time on this trip I've felt I was in Biblical times either, that's for sure!

Joseph took us to an area where a large pelican that he named Johnny was swimming and surprisingly got him to come over to the boat and to open his very large beak!

Then, to my particular delight, we headed to Crescent Island which was literally shaped like a crescent moon and was another location "Out of Africa" was filmed. Privately owned and occupied, the owner's home was the only building on the island.

The sun going down and the mountains behind it offered a glorious view. I stared at it, wondering what scenes may have been done there. I couldn't believe how close I've been to so many of the significant spots of filming.

The last leg of the hippo tour included a fun surprise — two hippos were on the shore eating! We got fairly close and enjoyed watching them have their dinner. The staff mowers had left them a pile of freshly cut grass which they love. They are humungous, weighing approximately four thousand pounds each!

Joseph told us they were relaxed with us there, otherwise they would have stopped chewing and gotten very still. He explained we were better off in the water then someone coming from the other direction on land would be. That would bother the hippos more.

We really enjoyed the view. They were such odd looking creatures. I've learned so much on this trip it's genuinely hard to take it all in. We turned in our life jackets and headed back to our tents. I packed up for the trip home before dinner.

Oddly, it felt like we had been gone longer than twelve days but at the same time seemed too soon to be getting ready to go. America seemed like a stranger to me now. I had not talked to my kids (or anyone else for that matter) in so long it was disorienting.

Today Justin was to get Pebble to the vet to have her front claws removed. He was headed to Boy Scout Camp last I knew. I hoped all went smoothly for him staying at the house. And I wondered how Laura was acclimating to New York City by now.

It was all just bizarre. I haven't had cell service or wifi all this time. I was so disconnected from life at home, and this group of people had been my family for the last several days. We ate our last supper together. It was scrumptious. My favorite was the fried zucchini. Maybe I will cook differently when I get home. I just didn't know how being here was going to affect my life from now on. Time will tell.

Rest...

One more day...

Goodnight, Africa.

Day 13

Our last morning in Africa was here, and I was having mixed feelings for sure. Although I missed some things about home and definitely wanted to speak to the kids, I also had a hard time imagining walking away from this experience. The sun was shining at least, and we had something new to do today — we were visiting a couple of orphanages. But first, we packed up and ate breakfast.

We had another good meal and started out. The first stop was the Osborne Library to see the paint job that had been completed this week and then picked up food to deliver to the orphanages.

We were surprised to see our little friends Susan, Eunice, Isaac and Eric not in school but instead hanging out there. Susan explained her mother had to go to a funeral out of town today, so she had to stay home from school.

I asked her about the death and she replied, "He was a young man, just twenty-two."

"Oh my gosh, Susan, what happened to him?" I asked.

"His throat was cut and his body chopped into pieces," she nonchalantly stated.

I was mortified that this little nine year old girl had even been given this information, let alone listening to her say these things out loud as if this were not unusual. (Maybe it wasn't unusual?) At least she didn't know him personally, apparently.

But, Debbie and I decided to stay with the kids, sing songs and dance with them. Susan reminded me I was supposed to bring crackers when I visited next, but I told her I didn't realize she would be there.

We loaded up food, prayed as a group, then hugged the kids, giving them lots of messages about the importance of reading each day and staying in school as long as possible. We explained we were getting on the big plane tonight, so we knew we would not be seeing them again.

It was hard to leave them behind knowing somewhat what they will be dealing with growing up in Maai Mahiu. Susan said she had never been out of this town in her life. She hoped to attend a university outside of Kenya. I encouraged her to hold onto that dream. And then we <u>had</u> to go.

We proceeded down the road to the first orphanage, Beat the Drum, which currently houses twenty-seven HIV positive orphans. They have been open for eight years, run by Pastor Peter and his wife Josephine. They had three biological children, one of whom we met (Esther), and they had adopted Mary, who came to the orphanage HIV positive at one month old and was now quite healthy at age one year.

Most of the children were in school when we arrived, but some of the teens had tests and were on a different schedule, so we got to meet them. We had tea together and lovely visits. We took a group picture with the stack of food.

Later while inside her living room, I asked Josephine how long the food would last that we had brought to them. A big smile formed on her face as she excitedly exclaimed, "You gave us a huge gift today. This food will last the children six months!"

That small pile would last six months? How is that possible? I wondered in that moment how big a food pile would have to be to feed twenty-seven American children for half a year. Would it all fit in my double car garage, or would we need my entire driveway for such a pile?

I noticed lots of clothes being laid over the bushes to dry. There are no dryers in Kenya. (This is why our towels were always a bit damp each day at the camp even though they were clean.) A crew was there to build a new kitchen for the orphanage, so that was an exciting development.

Our stay was brief but meaningful. I was so thankful for a glimpse of this life and ministry, and so happy to be able to praise them for the very special work they were doing there. The kids all looked healthy and strong, they were doing well in school and were also very kind which was impressive and heartwarming to say the least.

We went to the next orphanage. This one was much larger with over 175 children who lived and attended school there. It's called Prayers Beyond Boundaries. Apparently, many of these children were orphaned from a civil war that occurred about five years ago. The war broke out due to a political election believed by some to be rigged, so a general slaughtering of civilians resulted. Incomprehensible. Devastating. Unimaginable.

We took a pile of food to them as well. They greeted us with song which was very sweet. There was always some kind of hospitality offered wherever we went, and the appreciation we received was unmatched. Everyone also prayed for us and shared their love.

After the "ceremony" we were allowed to mix with the children, gave them handshakes, high fives, or hugs. Some of them really hugged tightly, and I tried so hard to put a lot of motherly love into each embrace. I learned their names, looked them in the eye, and offered them my full attention.

I asked them what their dreams were, and so many of them said they wanted to be teachers, lawyers, and doctors. I hope they keep their goals high. No doubt they have good excuses not to, but it appeared they loved their home, school, and teachers. Not one child seemed to be feeling sorry for themselves, that's for sure. Incredible!

They gave us a tour all around. In their dorms, I noticed a sight no longer unusual to me. Each child had all their earthly possessions in one little plastic bag hanging on a nail. At least they each had a bed of their own too, unlike many children in the rural areas of Kenya.

They were raising chickens and rabbits and growing a large garden. This is all a part of their education and family life. They seemed joy-filled, healthy, and strong. Obviously, they feel loved and supported here. I was so impressed with everyone!

We were blessed in this visit and enjoyed it immensely. The kids were always hard to leave, even in good hands. They tugged at my heart so! They wanted us to stay and play ball, but time wouldn't allow it. We waved out the bus windows and blew kisses as long as we could, clear outside of the gate.

Back we rode to Camp Crescent for our final meal together. It was very nice, and one of the desserts was called the American

Brownie, but it wasn't like any brownie I've ever had. The texture was softer and moister, with a fluffier height. Plus, powdered sugar was lightly sprinkled on top. Delicious!

Debbie and I took a very quick walk to Lake Naivasha for one last look before we departed for good. We thanked all the staff for their many kindnesses to us. They told us they would miss us and some took pictures.

This was also our moment to part from our team leaders, Joe Bob and Nyakio, as they were staying in Africa for an extended period. Joe Bob told me what a great job I had done, and that he loved me. I cried and cried. Lots of hugs. Nyakio said, "Oh, you're crying 'cause it's just so much," and I replied, "Yes, that's exactly it." She understands. She's been through this with many groups over the years.

Our trip to the airport was a bit long but full of our last beautiful views of Africa. I stared and stared at Mount Longonot and all the trees and terrain around. We got our last glimpses of zebras and giraffes which was a bittersweet treat along the way.

On the other hand, we also witnessed one of the most disturbing African sights yet. We drove past Kibera, the largest urban slum in Kenya, believed to be home of over a million people. The homes, made of whatever materials could be collected, were tiny, crammed with large families and looked like they could fall over at any moment. Many lived without access to clean water, electricity, or any kind of employment. A high percentage of residents had AIDS. School was a luxury for only a few. When I asked how the people there survive at all, the response given was, "I have no idea."

What are we supposed to do?

Traffic was wild at times, with lots of trucks barely able to climb the hills and oncoming vehicles crazy and fast as usual. I was thankful I never had to drive here and will not miss this aspect of the trip.

We stopped just a bit before the airport for an early supper together. While we ate, I took in the sun, fresh air, and good company with these folks as the final hours were rapidly ticking away.

A few miles later we arrived at the airport and said, "So long," to Bob who headed to England and Nancy who headed to Portugal. The other seven of us stayed together until we got to Kansas City.

Security at the Nairobi airport began outside the airport, as we had to depart the bus, walk through a short security building, then return to the bus. Lots of guards stood all around with guns.

The bus took us to our terminal, and the next series of security checks began. All the airport staff seemed kind and patient, but there were security checkpoints so often and so repetitive I wondered how any criminal or scheming passenger could ever get through. I guess that was the point!

Our gate was closed until two hours before our flight, so we had lots of free time to roam around, but other than one small food court, a couple of shops, and a coffee place, there wasn't much to do or places to be.

We went on walks and visited the *vyoo* (bathroom) quite often due to all the fluids we were drinking. We took up residence in the coffee house for quite a long while and enjoyed visiting.

Finally we proceeded to the gate but all carry-ons had to be sniffed by dogs, and a security person checked our passports once more. Wow!

At midnight, our plane lifted us out of Africa, and I couldn't help but feel a bit relieved and melancholy all at the same time. I realized I hadn't even begun to wrap my brain around everything I had seen, done, and learned. What a life-changing couple of weeks it had been.

Goodnight, Africa.

Day 14

I slept some on the plane after we reached altitude and had been fed a good meal. I was pretty comfortable throughout the night, although I had found most flights a bit chilly. Morning came and when they served us breakfast, we remembered to keep up our malaria pill-taking routine, which had to continue another five days after we returned.

We landed in Amsterdam on schedule but only had about an hour between flights and as it turned out, lots of security checkpoints there to get through. Again, everyone was kind, but it took so much time we couldn't even use the bathroom or we wouldn't have been on time for boarding. That was a little distressing when we had been stuck on a plane for nine hours.

So, with hardly knowing we had been in Europe again, we were back on another plane for another nine hour flight. The staff was kind and attentive. We were well-cared for and kept pretty well-hydrated, fed, and comfortable. We were just a bit chilly all the time, even with sleeves and blankets to cuddle up with.

I rested some but had a bit of diarrhea and wondered if my body was adjusting back to more "typical" food for me now? Who knows, but I only felt queasy for a time, and then I was fine again.

I watched two movies on the plane I'd been wanting to see which was fun and helped pass the time: "Joy" a true story of a woman's rags-to-riches story, and "The Lady in the Van" another true story about a homeless woman who lived in a British gentleman's driveway for fifteen years. Very fascinating and a bit ironic after the two weeks I had just experienced, both movies delighted and inspired me. I thought to myself, could I possibly inspire people in my life too? Hmmm...

I rested some and enjoyed visiting with my fellow travelers more. Debbie and I looked at her pictures and reflected on some of our experiences.

Later in the flight, I had a period of overwhelm hit, and my emotions took over. There was just so much to absorb from this experience. I imagined I would be processing all of this for a very long time.

Finally, we landed on American soil in Atlanta, Georgia — WOW! I felt it had been much longer than two weeks since I left the country. Anyway, we immediately headed to Customs.

First we had to go to kiosks to get a special document printed out from scanning our passport and taking our photo. Then we went through another security line, then another, then to get our baggage, then to reclaim our baggage and then through the usual security checkpoints.

My carry-on required a special search, and I was frisked. I had some gifts wrapped in newspaper from Africa and a glass jar of applesauce for Justin which was wrapped in a pair of my socks. So embarrassing, but oh well. At least the socks had not been worn. I didn't have any dignity left after thirty hours of travel anyway.

The TSA agent was kind, had a good sense of humor, and let me keep everything.

Finally, we were all in the clear and rode the train to our terminal and found our gate.

I was super happy to be able to use my phone at last, especially to connect with the kids! YAY! I will call them tonight from home but quickly texted them at the airport.

I was also happy to have some text messages waiting for me to find. Felt so good having friends check in, so I took time to reconnect with each who had reached out, and they all seemed very happy to know I was back in the United States. This felt so great, especially since I was not coming home to a spouse or anything. Yet I was surrounded by love and care all the time.

And now I had gained a whole new set of friends from the Kansas to Kenya organization and in Africa! It's amazing how my circle continues to broaden. When we open ourselves up to new experiences, places, and people, this is the sweetest blessing.

We walked a bit around the airport and enjoyed picking some food to eat without having to think about any particular "restrictions" to protect ourselves as we had in Africa. We were so tired and eager to finish our travels.

Felt pretty cool to board the plane with just the boarding pass as well. Life was returning to normalcy one step at a time; although I had a feeling my "normal" would change from having done this mission trip.

I was so thankful. I felt so blessed.

We boarded our final flight to realize for the first time ever, none of us were seated together. The flight was full also, so we didn't bother to try to switch around. Maybe this was God's way (or the travel agent's) to begin to wean us away from each other which was required when we landed in Kansas City anyway. Maybe this naturally built in some time for quiet, personal reflection while still in the travel phase.

Whatever the reason, we were all on board, in our own individual seats, no doubt each contemplating how our futures would be altered by where we had just been, all we had seen, and what we had done.

Two short hours later, we landed in Kansas City. We unceremoniously headed to baggage claim, some of our group being greeted by loved ones along the way, a series of happy reunions indeed. As we waited for the bags to begin their final journey to us, I looked around the carousel and found every remaining K2K member I had come to love and appreciate.

I briefly stared at each of them, realizing I had only known most of them for a very short time, but quickly grew to admire them and how they had chosen to use their gifts, talents, and resources for others. I had never been good at saying goodbye to people or ending a unique experience with others, and today would not be an exception.

I made sure I saw each one, hugged them, thanked them, and wished them well. We reminded each other we would gather some time in the next few months for a team reunion. This eased the emotional blow of the moment somewhat. Parting really was such sweet sorrow.

I think for me, parting from them was particularly difficult, because these are the only people that will always truly understand my feelings and experiences. They are the ones who know what I now know. I was daunted by the thought of trying to explain all of this to those who haven't been to Kenya or any other third world country for that matter. Yet I felt a deep responsibility to do so.

I got in John's car again, just as I had two weeks before, only this time with a tired body, no more anticipation, and a strange array of emotions I had no idea what to do with. As we headed north on Interstate 29 toward Atchison, I realized it was bedtime in Kenya.

Goodnight, Africa.

Day 1

Back Home

Pulling into my driveway near the back door, John stopped the car and began to unload my bags from his trunk. After quickly hugging and thanking his wife for the ride, my eyes met his, and I wondered how I would ever be able to express my gratitude enough to this man who had invited me on this journey. Starting off as acquaintances for many years, then shifting into friendship in the last six months, now he had become more like a father figure to me. Hugging him tightly, I couldn't find any words at all. My throat tightened, the tears began to well up, and I hesitantly pulled myself away from him.

Protective to the end, he waited to make sure my door unlocked, and I had made it inside my home before driving away. I shut the door behind me and dragged my bags down the steps and stopped. All was quiet here. Laura was in New York City, Justin at Camp Geiger, and Pebble at the vet's office recovering from being declawed.

I walked into the kitchen and opened the refrigerator and freezer doors annoyed and overwhelmed. Of course, the shelves were bare. That's what happens when you go away for a while. Heading over to the pantry next, I anticipated finding the same emptiness. I did.

While whining inside my head about being too tired to go to the grocery store, a new perspective came to my consciousness. "Put your Africa eyes on, Cindy, and look again," said The Voice.

Back to the refrigerator I went, opened the doors and saw a little bit of milk, six eggs, some cheese, frozen beans, and frozen corn. In the pantry, two cans of soup, three kinds of pasta, a jar of sauce, a half of a box of cereal, more tea bags than I would use in three months, two kinds of crackers, oatmeal, peanut butter, and some protein bars all stared back at me.

My American self thought my cupboards were bare, and it was time to stock up at the store. My new African eyes realized there was more than enough to eat in this house. Many of the people I had spent the past two weeks with would have felt they had found the food jackpot in my house, yet I was initially feeling in short supply.

I promised myself not to go to the store until it became "necessary" and for the next four days ate happily, three full meals per day, plus snacks in between, never experiencing even five minutes of hunger. By the time I did go to the store, I honestly could have kept eating at home for some time, but I decided I had learned my lesson, had nothing left to drink in the house but tea and water, and having fresh produce again for the first time in weeks would be nice.

After I finished eating my first meal back at home, I called each of my children. Hearing their voices and knowing all was well with them was a huge comfort.

I walked from room to room in my house, a small (by American standards), fourteen hundred square foot tri-level place I had purchased following my divorce four years ago.

Although I had thought I was a simple, nonmaterialistic person generally speaking, I realized I had more space and owned more things than almost every Kenyan person I had met on this trip. My kids and I felt this "cottage" (as we affectionately call it) was perfect for the three of us. In Kenya, eight to ten people would likely live in a space the size of just our living room. How could I go on living this way when I knew so many people had so little? The lack of balance was so unsettling.

Physically and emotionally exhausted, I decided to head to the bathtub to relax, unwind, and get clean. Turning on the hot water, I robotically added lavender scented bubble bath as I've done hundreds of times before, filled my tall glass of ice water and lit a beautiful candle. I removed the clothes I had been wearing for the past thirty-six hours and sank into the luscious bubbles and steamy water.

Closing my eyes, I basked in the luxuriousness of it all. Ahhhhhh — this felt so wonderful.

Suddenly, my eyes popped wide open and I was mortified. How could I be so insensitive? How could I be so selfish? Who do I think I am? Who am I to just "waste" some fifty gallons of hot, clean water for my personal pleasure when I JUST got off a plane from a place where even a drip of clean, cold water was difficult to find?

The tears streamed down my face, and I apologized out loud to whom I don't even actually know, and although bathing had been one of my all time favorite forms of relaxation for years, I could barely stand to remain in this setting. The guilt just consumed me.

After my meltdown, still in the tub, I realized continuing to bathe wasn't going to change the circumstances of my dear African friends in any way, shape, or form, positively or negatively. Whether I went to the store tomorrow or next week wasn't going to change anything for them either. If I sold all my material possessions that didn't seem "absolutely necessary" that wouldn't help either.

Before laying down to sleep back in my cozy bed, I dug into my suitcase and found my toothbrush. I unconsciously walked into the bathroom, squeezed the toothpaste on it, and ran water directly out of a faucet on it for the first time in two weeks. As I scrubbed my teeth, my eyes looked up into the mirror and soon I saw not just my face, but the faces of those precious women I had given a new toothbrush to just days ago, and I wondered if they would remember my face each time they used it.

Would they, could they, believe that their American sister was thinking of them now, even as she was returning to the comforts of her own land? Would they be able to call upon the strength, wisdom, and genuine love I had attempted to share with them especially when they were having a difficult day? Would they believe that I would always remember them no matter what, just like I promised I would?

And what about the children? As the years continue, will they remember the day I sang songs on the grass with them? Will they have a bit more confidence and determination to live differently because of our time together? Will they feel my hugs when they are lonely?

Will the abused young women never again engage in an unhealthy relationship? Will the families at Badilika manage their alcoholism in a more healthy way? Will the executive directors of the nonprofit agencies learn to cooperate with one another? Will all my new friends in Africa realize I will forever care for them whether we cross paths again or not?

And how do I go on living with myself, knowing how little some in our world have while I can get anything I need at any time? There isn't any particular reason I know of that I just "happened" to be born in a middle class American family as opposed to an African family in a poverty stricken, third world country.

Thoughts like these continued to consume me upon my return, and I found myself flattened by them doing very, very little for the first few days. Part of the adjustment to returning from a trip overseas is acclimating to the time change and getting back on a regular sleep schedule. I expected those things.

What I hadn't anticipated was a kind of survivor guilt, the feeling of being overly privileged without a really good reason or explanation for my good fortune in life. Not even being able to brush my teeth without pondering some of the most gripping problems of the world at the same time. I used to think choosing the right clothes for a specific occasion, saving a specific amount of money for retirement, being on time, constantly "achieving," and losing the extra thirty pounds I had been emotionally torturing myself over for most of my adult life REALLY mattered.

But what ACTUALLY matters?

Love.
Kindness.
Peace.
Hope.
Faith.
Joy.
Respect.
People.
Animals.
All living things.
Giving.
Serving.
Caring.
Forgiving.
Understanding.
Being.
Awareness.
Honesty.
Living fully.
Doing what you can do when you know something needs to be done.

And on and on this list could go.

Explaining this mission trip and my response to everything has been a daunting honor that brings tears to my eyes and chips away at my soul a bit every single time. Even months later, I am tossing and turning thoughts, memories, and ideas in my head and heart about what all of this means and what I am meant to do now that I have seen another view of the world we all share.

What I know for sure is, when we realize a need exists for another, whether it is our next-door neighbor, someone we live with, a family member, a colleague, a friend, or our brothers and sisters somewhere in the world that we may not ever even meet, we have a <u>deep</u> responsibility to offer what we have been given to support them in their journey.

No matter what our life story is, no matter where we've been or what we've experienced, none of us have ever made our way totally alone.

My deepest desire is that I may continue to be used in service to the greater good of humanity with my unique gifts, talents, and resources as long as I live, and that you will too.

Asante Sona (Thank you very much), Africa.

To contact the author regarding speaking engagements or other services, go to www.cindydwhitmer.com.

For more information about Kansas to Kenya, please visit www.kansas2kenya.com.

For more information about Agatha Amani House, please visit www.agathaamanihouse.org *or* www.empoweringmindsinternational.org.

A portion of your purchase will be donated to these organizations.